Plant Based Diet Cookbook for Beginners 2021

A Step-by-Step Cookbook To Make Delicious Low
Carb Plant Based Dishes For Whole Family

Jennifer Smith

By reading this document, the reader agrees that under no circumstances is the author responsible for any losses, direct or indirect, which are incurred as a result of the use of information contained within this document, including, but not limited to, errors, omissions, or inaccuracies.

Table Of Content

BREAKFAST & SMOOTHIES

Pumpkin Smoothie

Preparation time: 5 minutes

Servings 2

Ingredients:

- 1 cup unsweetened non-dairy milk
- 2 medium bananas, peeled and cut into quarters and frozen
- 2 medjool dates, pitted
- 1 cup pumpkin puree, canned or fresh
- 2 cups ice cubes
- ¼ tsp cinnamon
- 2 tbsp ground flaxseeds
- 1 tsp pumpkin spice

Directions:

Blend all ingredients in a blender and serve.

Nutrition:

Calories 272, Total Fat 5.6g, Saturated Fat 2.2g, Cholesterol 10mg, Sodium 75mg, Total Carbohydrate 51.9g, Dietary Fiber 9.5g,Total Sugars 29.4g, Protein 8.2g, Vitamin D 1mcg, Calcium 204mg, Iron 4mg,Potassium 865mg

__Date Chocolate Smoothie__

Preparation Time: 5 minutes

Servings: 2

Ingredients

- Unsweetened cocoa powder: 2 tbsp
- Unsweetened nut milk: 2 cups
- Almond butter: 2 tbsp
- Dried dates: 4 pitted
- Frozen bananas: 2 medium
- Ground cinnamon: ¼ tsp

Directions:

1. Add all the ingredients to the blender
2. Blend to form a smooth consistency

Nutrition:

Carbs: 72.1 g

Protein: 8 g

Fats: 12.7 g

Calories: 385 Kcal

Very Berry Smoothie

Preparation time: 5 minutes

Servings 2

Ingredients:

- 2 cups, plant-based Milk
- 2 cups, Frozen or fresh berries
- ½ cup Frozen ripe bananas
- 2 teaspoons, Flax Seeds
- ¼ tsp, Vanilla
- ¼ tsp, Cinnamon

Directions:

1. Mix together milk, flax seeds, and fruit. Blend in a high-power blender.
2. Add cinnamon and vanilla. Blend until smooth.
3. Serve and enjoy!

Nutrition:

Calories 269, Total Fat 12.3g, Saturated Fat 2.3g, Cholesterol 0mg, Sodium 312mg, Total Carbohydrate 37.6g, Dietary Fiber 8.2g, Total Sugars 22.9g, Protein 6.4g, Vitamin D 0mcg, Calcium 52mg, Iron 3mg, Potassium 528mg

Peppermint Monster Smoothie

Preparation time: 5 minutes

Servings 1

Ingredients:

- 1 large frozen banana, peeled
- 1½ cups non-dairy milk
- A handful of fresh mint leaves, stems removed
- 1-2 handfuls spinach

Directions:

1. Add all ingredients in a blender and blend until smooth.
2. Take out and serve

Nutrition:

Calories 799, Total Fat 28.1g, Saturated Fat 16.7g, Cholesterol 110mg   , Sodium 645mg, Total Carbohydrate 98.4g, Dietary Fiber 4.5g, Total Sugars 77.2g, Protein 46.2g,   Vitamin D 7mcg, Calcium 1634mg, Iron 2mg, Potassium 1366mg

Veggie Smoothie

Preparation time: 10 minutes

Servings 1

Ingredients:

- 1 stalk celery
- 1 carrot peeled and roughly chopped
- ½ cup broccoli sprouts
- 1 cup kale, chopped
- ½ cup curly parsley
- ½ tomato roughly chopped
- ½ avocado
- 1 banana
- ½ green apple
- ½ cup non-dairy milk
- 1 tbsp chia seeds
- 1 tbsp flaxseeds

Directions:

1. Place all ingredients in a blender.
2. Blend until smooth. Serve immediately.

Nutrition:

Calories 696, Total Fat 34.1g, Saturated Fat 7g, Cholesterol 10mg, Sodium 190mg, Total Carbohydrate 90.5g, Dietary Fiber 29.5g, Total Sugars 37.2g,   Protein 18.5g, Vitamin D 1mcg, Calcium 527mg, Iron 9mg, Potassium 2223mg

Cinnamon Coffee Shake

Preparation time: 5 minutes

Servings 2

Ingredients:

- 1 cup cooled coffee, regular or decaf
- ¼ cup almond or non-dairy milk
- A few pinches cinnamon
- 2 tbsp hemp seeds
- Splash vanilla extract
- 2 frozen bananas, sliced into coins
- Handful of ice

Directions:

1. Chill some coffee in a sealed container for a couple of hours (or overnightbefore making this smoothie, or be ready to use more ice.
2. Add the non-dairy milk, cinnamon, vanilla, and hemp seeds to a blender and blend until smooth. Add the coffee and cut bananas and keep blending until smooth.
3. Add the ice and keep blending on high until there are no lumps remaining. Taste for sweetness and add your

preferred plant-based sugar or sugar alternative.

4. Transfer to a glass and serve.

Nutrition:

Calories 197, Total Fat 6.4g, Saturated Fat 0.6g, Cholesterol 0mg, Sodium 5mg, Total Carbohydrate 31.3g, Dietary Fiber 5.2g, Total Sugars 15.8g, Protein 4g,   Vitamin D 0mcg, Calcium 53mg, Iron 1mg, Potassium 582mg

Banana Green Smoothie

Preparation time: 5 minutes

Servings 1

Ingredients:

- 1 cup coconut water
- ¾ cup plant-based milk
- ¼ tsp vanilla extract
- 1 heaping cup loosely packed spinach
- 2-3 cups frozen bananas, sliced

Directions:

Blend everything until smooth and serve.

Nutrition:

Calories 364, Total Fat 4.8g, Saturated Fat 2.6g, Cholesterol 15mg, Sodium 111mg, Total Carbohydrate 78g, Dietary Fiber 8g, Total Sugars 45.1g, Protein 9.6g, Vitamin D 1mcg, Calcium 257mg, Iron 1mg, Potassium 1241mg

Date Banana Pistachio Smoothie

Preparation Time: 5 minutes

Servings: 4

Ingredients

- Pistachios: 1 cup
- Raw pumpkin:175 g
- Cloves:1
- Nutmeg:1/8 tsp
- Dates: 4
- Banana:1
- Ground ginger:1/8 tsp
- Ground cinnamon:1 tsp
- Cashew milk:500 ml
- *Ice:* as per your need

Directions:

1. Add all the ingredients to the blender
2. Blend on high speed to make it smooth

Nutrition:

Carbs: 32.9 g

Protein: 9.7 g

Fats: 15 g

Calories: 320 Kcal

Turmeric Smoothie

Preparation time: 5 minutes

Servings 2

Ingredients:

- 2 cups non-dairy milk like coconut, almond
- 2 medium bananas, frozen
- 1 cup mango, frozen
- 1 tsp turmeric, ground grated, peeled
- 1 tsp fresh ginger, grated, peeled
- 1 tbsp chia seeds
- ¼ tsp vanilla extract
- ¼ tsp cinnamon, ground
- 1 pinch pepper, ground

Directions:

Blend all ingredients in a blender and serve

Nutrition:

Calories 785, Total Fat 62.4g, Saturated Fat 51.5g, Cholesterol 0mg, Sodium 41mg, Total Carbohydrate 60.2g, Dietary Fiber 15g, Total Sugars 33.9g, Protein 10g, Vitamin D 0mcg, Calcium 149mg, Iron 6mg, Potassium 1292mg

Orange Smoothie

Preparation time: 5 minutes

Servings 2

Ingredients:

- 1 cup orange slices
- 1 cup mango chunks
- 1 cup strawberries, chopped
- 1 cup coconut water
- Pinch freshly grated ginger
- 1-2 cups crushed ice

Directions:

Place everything in a blender, blend, and serve.

Nutrition:

Calories 269, Total Fat 12.3g, Saturated Fat 2.3g, Cholesterol 0mg, Sodium 312mg, Total Carbohydrate 37.6g, Dietary Fiber 8.2g, Total Sugars 22.9g, Protein 6.4g, Vitamin D 0mcg, Calcium 52mg, Iron 3mg, Potassium 528mg

Coco Loco Smoothie

Preparation Time: 5 minutes

Servings: 2

Ingredients

- Coconut milk: 1 cup
- Frozen cauliflower florets: ½ cup
- Frozen mango cubes: 1 cup
- Almond butter: 1 tbsp

Directions:

1. Add all the ingredients to the blender
2. Blend on high speed to make it smooth

Nutrition:

Carbs: 18.2 g

Protein: 10.2 g

Fats: 27.0 g

Calories: 309 Kcal

Creamy Carrot Smoothie

Preparation Time: 5 minutes

Servings: 4

Ingredients

- Almond milk: 2 cups
- Prunes: 60 g
- Banana: 1
- Carrots: 150 g
- Walnuts: 30 g
- Ground cinnamon:½ tsp
- Vanilla extract:1 tsp
- Ground nutmeg:¼ tsp

Directions:

1. Add all the ingredients to the blender
2. Blend on high speed to make it smooth

Nutrition:

Carbs: 14.9 g

Protein: 3 g

Fats: 4.5 g

Calories: 103 Kcal

MAINS

Curried Tofu Meatballs

Preparation Time: 5 minutes

Cooking Time: 25 minutes

Servings: 4

Ingredients:

- 3 lb ground tofu
- 1 medium yellow onion, finely chopped
- 2 green bell peppers, deseeded and chopped
- 3 garlic cloves, minced
- 2 tbsp melted butter
- 1 tsp dried parsley
- 2 tbsp hot sauce
- Salt and ground black pepper to taste
- 1 tbsp red curry powder
- 3 tbsp olive oil

Directions:

1. Preheat the oven to 400 F and grease a baking sheet with cooking spray.
2. In a bowl, combine the tofu, onion, bell peppers, garlic, butter, parsley, hot sauce, salt, black pepper, and curry powder. With your hands, form 1-inch tofu ball from the mixture and place on the greased baking sheet.
3. Drizzle the olive oil over the meat and bake in the oven until the tofu ball brown on the outside and Cooking Time: within, 20 to 25 minutes.

4. Remove the dish from the oven and plate the tofu ball.

5. Garnish with some scallions and serve warm on a bed of spinach salad with herbed vegan paneer cheese dressing.

Nutrition:

Calories:506, Total Fat:45.6g, Saturated Fat:18.9g, Total Carbs:11g, Dietary Fiber:1g, Sugar:1g, Protein:19g, Sodium:794mg

Cheesy Mushroom Pie

Preparation Time: 12minutes

Cooking Time: 43minutes

Servings: 4

Ingredients:

For the piecrust:

- ¼ cup almond flour + extra for dusting
- 3 tbsp coconut flour
- ½ tsp salt
- ¼ cup butter, cold and crumbled
- 3 tbsp erythritol
- 1 ½ tsp vanilla extract
- 4 whole eggs

For the filling:

- 2 tbsp butter
- 1 medium yellow onion
- 2 garlic cloves, minced
- 2 cups mixed mushrooms, chopped
- 1 green bell pepper, deseeded and diced
- 1 cup green beans, cut into 3 pieces each
- Salt and black pepper to taste
- ¼ cup coconut creaminutes
- 1/3 cup vegan sour creaminutes
- ½ cup almond milk

- 2 eggs, lightly beaten
- ¼ tsp nutmeg powder
- 1 tbsp chopped parsley
- 1 cup grated parmesan cheese

Directions:

For the pastry crust:

1. Preheat the oven to 350 F and grease a pie pan with cooking spray
2. In a large bowl, mix the almond flour, coconut flour, and salt.
3. Add the butter and mix with an electric hand mixer until crumbly. Add the erythritol and vanilla extract until mixed in. Then, pour in the eggs one after another while mixing until formed into a ball.
4. Flatten the dough a clean flat surface, cover in plastic wrap, and refrigerate for 1 hour.
5. After, lightly dust a clean flat surface with almond flour, unwrap the dough, and roll out the dough into a large rectangle, ½ - inch thickness and fit into a pie pan.
6. Pour some baking beans onto the pastry and bake in the oven until golden. Remove after, pour the beans, and allow cooling.

For the filling:

1. Meanwhile, melt the butter in a skillet and sauté the onion and garlic until softened and fragrant, 3 minutes.

Add the mushrooms, bell pepper, green beans, salt and black pepper; Cooking Time: for 5 minutes.

2. In a medium bowl, beat the coconut cream, vegan sour cream, milk, and eggs. Season with black pepper, salt, and nutmeg. Stir in the parsley and cheese.

3. Spread the mushroom mixture in the baked pastry and spread the cheese filling on top. Place the pie in the oven and bake for 30 to 35 minutes or until a toothpick inserted into the pie comes out clean and golden on top.

4. Remove, let cool for 10 minutes, slice, and serve with roasted tomato salad.

Nutrition:

Calories:120, Total Fat:9.2g, Saturated Fat:2.3g, Total Carbs:7g, Dietary Fiber:3g, Sugar:3g, Protein:5g, Sodium:17mg

Zucchini Seitan Stacks

Preparation Time: 15 minutes

Cooking Time: 18 minutes

Servings: 4

Ingredients:

- 1 ½ lb seitan
- 3 tbsp almond flour
- Salt and black pepper to taste
- 2 large zucchinis, cut into 2-inch slices
- 4 tbsp olive oil
- 2 tsp Italian mixed herb blend
- ½ cup vegetable broth

Directions:

1. Preheat the oven to 400 F.
2. Cut the seitan into strips and set aside.
3. In a zipper bag, add the almond flour, salt, and black pepper. Mix and add the seitan slices. Seal the bag and shake to coat the seitan with the seasoning.
4. Grease a baking sheet with cooking spray and arrange the zucchinis on the baking sheet. Season with salt and black pepper, and drizzle with 2 tablespoons of olive oil.
5. Using tongs, remove the seitan from the almond flour mixture, shake off the excess flour, and put two to three seitan strips on each zucchini.

6. Season with the herb blend and drizzle again with olive oil.

7. Cooking Time: in the oven for 8 minutes; remove the sheet and carefully pour in the vegetable broth. Bake further for 5 to 10 minutes or until the seitan cooks through.

8. Remove from the oven and serve warm with low carb bread.

Nutrition:

Calories:582, Total Fat:49.7g, Saturated Fat:18.4g, Total Carbs:8g, Dietary Fiber:3g, Sugar:2g, Protein:31g, Sodium:385mg

Spicy Mushroom Collard Wraps

Preparation Time: 10 minutes

Cooking Time: 16 minutes

Servings: 4

Ingredients:

- 2 tbsp avocado oil
- 1 large yellow onion, chopped
- 2 garlic cloves, minced
- Salt and ground black pepper to taste
- 1 small jalapeño pepper, deseeded and finely chopped
- 1 ½ lb mushrooms, cut into 1-inch cubes
- 1 cup cauliflower rice
- 2 tsp hot sauce
- 8 collard leaves
- ¼ cup plain unsweetened yogurt for topping

Directions:

1. Heat 2 tablespoons of avocado oil in a large deep skillet; add and sauté the onion until softened, 3 minutes.
2. Pour in the garlic, salt, black pepper, and jalapeño pepper; Cooking Time: until fragrant, 1 minute.
3. Mix in the mushrooms and Cooking Time: both sides, 10 minutes.
4. Add the cauliflower rice, and hot sauce. Sauté until the cauliflower slightly softens, 2 to 3 minutes. Adjust the taste with salt and black pepper.

5. Lay out the collards on a clean flat surface and spoon the curried mixture onto the middle part of the leaves, about 3 tablespoons per leaf. Spoon the plain yogurt on top, wrap the leaves, and serve immediately.

Nutrition:

Calories:380, Total Fat:34.8g, Saturated Fat:19.9g, Total Carbs:10g, Dietary Fiber:5g, Sugar:5g, Protein:10g, Sodium:395mg

Creamy Fettucine With Peas

Preparation Time: 25 minutes

Serving: 4

This one is a dish made to taste fantastic. The tip for success is covering or coating the noodles in so much lushness.

Ingredients

- 16 oz whole-wheat fettuccine
- Salt and black pepper to taste
- ¾ cup flax milk
- ½ cup cashew butter, room temperature
- 1 tbsp olive oil
- 2 garlic cloves, minced
- 1 ½ cups frozen peas
- ½ cup chopped fresh basil

Directions

1. Add the fettuccine and 10 cups of water to a large pot, and Cooking Time: over medium heat until al dente, 10 minutes. Drain the pasta through a colander and set aside. In a bowl, whisk the flax milk, cashew butter, and salt until smooth. Set aside.

2. Heat the olive oil in a large skillet and sauté the garlic until fragrant, 30 seconds. Mix in the peas, fettuccine, and basil. Toss well until the pasta is well-coated in the sauce and season with some black pepper. Dish the food and serve warm.

Nutrition:

Calories 654

Fats 23.7g| Carbs 101.9g

Protein 18.2g

Seitan Pesto Panini

Preparation Time: 15 minutes + 30 minutes refrigeration

Serving: 4

This is a delicious panini made from all plant sources.

Ingredients

For the seitan:

- 2/3 cup basil pesto
- ½ lemon, juiced
- 1 garlic clove, minced
- 1/8 tsp salt
- 1 cup chopped seitan

For the panini:

- 3 tbsp basil pesto
- 8 thick slices whole-wheat ciabatta
- Olive oil for brushing
- 8 slices plant-based mozzarella cheese
- 1 small yellow bell pepper, deseeded and chopped
- ¼ cup grated Parmesan cheese

Directions

For the seitan:

1. In a medium bowl, mix the pesto, lemon juice, garlic, and salt. Add the seitan and coat well with the marinade. Cover with a plastic wrap and marinate in the refrigerator for 30 minutes.

2. Preheat a large skillet over medium heat and remove the seitan from the fridge. Cooking Time: the seitan in the skillet until brown and cooked through, 2 to 3 minutes. Turn the heat off.

To make the panini:

1. Preheat a panini press to medium heat. In a small bowl, mix the pesto in the inner parts of two slices of bread. On the outer parts, apply some olive oil and place a slice with (the olive oil side downin the press.

2. Lay 2 slices of plant-based mozzarella cheese on the bread, spoon some seitan on top. Sprinkle with some bell pepper, and some plant-based Parmesan cheese. Cover with another bread slice.

3. Close the press and grill the bread for 1 to 2 minutes. Flip the bread, and grill further for 1 minute or until the cheese melts and golden brown on both sides. Serve warm.

Nutrition:

Calories 608

Fats 44.1g| Carbs 17g

Protein 37.6g

Mexican Quinoa And Lima Bean Bowls

Preparation Time: 30 minutes

Serving: 4

A bowl filled with Mexican flavors with lima beans and quinoa for the perfect combo! Full of flavors and spices.

Ingredients

- 1 tbsp olive oil
- 1 lb extra firm tofu, pressed and cut into 1-inch cubes
- Salt and black pepper to taste
- 1 medium yellow onion, finely diced
- ½ cup cauliflower florets
- 1 jalapeño pepper, minced
- 2 garlic cloves, minced
- 1 tbsp red chili powder
- 1 tsp cumin powder
- 1 (8 ozcan sweet corn kernels, drained
- 1 (8 ozcan lima beans, rinsed and drained
- 1 cup quick-cooking quinoa
- 1 (14 ozcan diced tomatoes
- 2 ½ cups vegetable broth
- 1 cup grated homemade plant-based cheddar cheese
- 2 tbsp chopped fresh cilantro
- 2 limes, cut into wedges for garnishing
- 1 medium avocado, pitted, sliced and peeled

Directions

1. Heat olive oil in a pot and Cooking Time: the tofu until golden brown, 5 minutes. Season with salt, pepper, and mix in onion, cauliflower, and jalapeño pepper. Cooking Time: until the vegetables soften, 3 minutes. Stir in garlic, chili powder, and cumin powder; Cooking Time: for 1 minute.

2. Mix in sweet corn kernels, lima beans, quinoa, tomatoes, and vegetable broth. Simmer until the quinoa absorbs all the liquid, 10 minutes. Fluff quinoa. Top with the plant-based cheddar cheese, cilantro, lime wedges, and avocado. Serve warm.

Nutrition:

Calories 414

Fats 20.3g| Carbs 45.9g

Protein 20.8g

Pesto Tofu Zoodles

Preparation Time: 5minutes

Cooking Time: 12minutes

Servings size 4

Ingredients:

- 2 tbsp olive oil
- 1 medium white onion, chopped
- 1 garlic clove, minced
- 2 (14 ozblocks firm tofu, pressed and cubed
- 1 medium red bell pepper, deseeded and sliced
- 6 medium zucchinis, spiralized
- Salt and black pepper to taste
- ¼ cup basil pesto, olive oil based
- 2/3 cup grated parmesan cheese
- ½ cup shredded mozzarella cheese
- Toasted pine nuts to garnish

Directions:

1. Heat the olive oil in a medium pot over medium heat; sauté the onion and garlic until softened and fragrant, 3 minutes.

2. Add the tofu and Cooking Time: until golden on all sides then pour in the bell pepper and Cooking Time: until softened, 4 minutes.

3. Mix in the zucchinis, pour the pesto on top, and season

with salt and black pepper. Cooking Time: for 3 to 4 minutes or until the zucchinis soften a little bit. Turn the heat off and carefully stir in the parmesan cheese.

4. Dish into four plates, share the mozzarella cheese on top, garnish with the pine nuts, and serve warm.

Nutrition:

Calories:79, Total Fat:6.2g, Saturated Fat:3.7g, Total Carbs:5g, Dietary Fiber:2g, Sugar:3g, Protein:2g, Sodium:54mg

Tofu Scallopini With Lemon

Preparation Time: 5minutes

Cooking Time: 21minutes

Servings: 4

Ingredients:

- 1½ lb thin cut tofu chops, boneless
- Salt and ground black pepper to taste
- 1 tbsp avocado oil
- 3 tbsp butter
- 2 tbsp capers
- 1 cup vegetable broth
- ½ lemon, juiced + 1 lemon, sliced
- 2 tbsp freshly chopped parsley

Directions:

1. Heat the avocado oil in a large skillet over medium heat. Season the tofu chops with salt and black pepper; Cooking Time: in the oil on both sides until brown and cooked through, 12 to 15 minutes. Transfer to a plate, cover with another plate, and keep warm.

2. Add the butter to the pan to melt and Cooking Time: the capers until hot and sizzling stirring frequently to avoid burning, 3 minutes.

3. Pour in the vegetable broth and lemon juice, use a

spatula to scrape any bits stuck to the bottom of the pan, and allow boiling until the sauce reduces by half.

4. Add the tofu back to the sauce, arrange the lemon slices on top, and sprinkle with half of the parsley. Allow simmering for 3 minutes.

5. Plate the food, garnish with the remaining parsley, and serve warm with creamy mashed cauliflower.

Nutrition:

Calories:214, Total Fat:15.6g, Saturated Fat:2.5g, Total Carbs:12g, Dietary Fiber:2g, Sugar:6g, Protein:9g, Sodium:280mg

Buckwheat Cabbage Rolls

Preparation Time: 30 minutes

Serving: 4

Ingredients

- 2 tbsp plant butter
- 2 cups extra firm tofu, pressed and crumbled
- ½ medium sweet onion, finely chopped
- 2 garlic cloves, minced
- Salt and black pepper to taste
- 1 cup buckwheat groats
- 1 ¾ cups vegetable stock
- 1 bay leaf
- 2 tbsp chopped fresh cilantro + more for garnishing
- 1 head Savoy cabbage, leaves separated (scraps kept)
- 1 (23 ozcanned chopped tomatoes

Directions

1. Melt the plant butter in a large bowl and Cooking Time: the tofu until golden brown, 8 minutes. Stir in the onion and garlic until softened and fragrant, 3 minutes. Season with salt, black pepper and mix in the buckwheat, bay leaf, and vegetable stock.

2. Close the lid, allow boiling, and then simmer until all the liquid is absorbed. Open the lid; remove the bay leaf, adjust the taste with salt, black pepper, and mix in

the cilantro.

3. Lay the cabbage leaves on a flat surface and add 3 to 4 tablespoons of the cooked buckwheat onto each leaf. Roll the leaves to firmly secure the filling.

4. Pour the tomatoes with juices into a medium pot, season with a little salt, black pepper, and lay the cabbage rolls in the sauce. Cooking Time: over medium heat until the cabbage softens, 5 to 8 minutes. Turn the heat off and dish the food onto serving plates. Garnish with more cilantro and serve warm.

Nutrition:

Calories 1147

Fats 112.9g| Carbs 25.6g

Protein 23.8g

Tofu Chops With Green Beans And Avocado Sauté

Preparation Time: 10minutes

Cooking Time: 22 minutes

Servings: 4

Ingredients:

For the tofu chops:

- 2 tbsp avocado oil
- 4 slices firm tofu
- Salt and ground black pepper to taste

For the green beans and avocado sauté:

- 2 tbsp avocado oil
- 1 ½ cups green beans
- 2 large avocados, halved, pitted, and chopped
- Salt and ground black pepper to taste
- 6 green onions, chopped
- 1 tbsp freshly chopped parsley

Directions:

For the tofu chops:

Heat the avocado oil in a medium skillet, season the tofu with salt and black pepper, and fry in the oil on both sides until brown, and cooked through, 12 to 15 minutes. Transfer to a plate and set aside in a warmer for serving.

For the green beans and avocado sauté:

1. Heat the avocado oil in a medium skillet, add and sauté

the green beans until sweating and slightly softened, 10 minutes. Mix in the avocados (don't worry if they mash up a bit), season with salt and black pepper, and the half of the green onions. Warm the avocados for 2 minutes. Turn the heat off.

2. Dish the sauté into serving plates, garnish with the remaining green onions and parsley, and serve with the tofu chops.

Nutrition:
Calories:503, Total Fat:41.9g, Saturated Fat:14.5g, Total Carbs:18g, Dietary Fiber:2g, Sugar:4g, Protein:19g, Sodium:314mg

Creole Tempeh Rice Bowls

Preparation Time: 50 minutes

Serving: 4

Tempeh with vegetable over rice makes it delicious and healthy.

Ingredients

- 2 tbsp olive oil
- 1 ½ cups crumbled tempeh
- 1 tsp Creole seasoning
- 2 red bell peppers, deseeded and sliced
- 1 cup brown rice
- 2 cups vegetable broth
- Salt to taste
- 1 lemon, zested and juiced
- 1 (8 ozcan black beans, drained and rinsed
- 2 chives, chopped
- 2 tbsp freshly chopped parsley

Directions

1. Heat the olive oil in a medium pot and Cooking Time: in the tempeh until golden brown, 5 minutes.
2. Season with the Creole seasoning and stir in the bell peppers. Cooking Time: until the peppers slightly soften, 3 minutes.
3. Stir in the brown rice, vegetable broth, salt, and lemon

zest.

4. Cover and Cooking Time: until the rice is tender and all the liquid is absorbed, 15 to 25 minutes.

5. Mix in the lemon juice, beans, and chives. Allow warming for 3 to 5 minutes and dish the food.

6. Garnish with the parsley and serve warm.

Nutrition:

Calories 216

Fats 13.9g| Carbs 13.8g

Protein 12.7g

SIDES AND SALADS

Roasted Bell Pepper Salad With Olives

Preparation Time: 10 minutes

Cooking Time: 20 minutes

Serving Size: 4

Ingredients:

- 8 large red bell peppers, deseeded and cut in wedges
- ½ tsp erythritol
- 2 ½ tbsp olive oil
- 1/3 cup arugula
- 1 tbsp mint leaves
- 1/3 cup pitted Kalamata olives
- 3 tbsp chopped almonds
- ½ tbsp balsamic vinegar
- Crumbled feta cheese for topping
- Toasted pine nuts for topping

Directions:

1. Preheat oven to 4000 F.
2. Pour bell peppers on a roasting pan; season with erythritol and drizzle with half of olive oil. Roast in oven until slightly charred, 20 minutes. Remove from oven and set aside.
3. Arrange arugula in a salad bowl, scatter bell peppers on top, mint leaves, olives, almonds, and drizzle with

balsamic vinegar and remaining olive oil. Season with salt and black pepper.

4. Toss; top with feta cheese and pine nuts and serve.

Nutrition:

Calories 163, Total Fat 13.3g, Total Carbs 6.53g, Fiber 2.2g, Net Carbs 4.33g, Protein 3.37g

Almond-Goji Berry Cauliflower Salad

Preparation Time: 10 minutes

Cooking Time: 2 minutes

Serving Size: 4

Ingredients:

- 1 small head cauliflower, cut into florets
- 8 sun-dried tomatoes in olive oil, drained
- 12 pitted green olives, roughly chopped
- 1 lemon, zested and juiced
- 3 tbsp chopped green onions
- A handful chopped almonds
- ¼ cup goji berries
- 1 tbsp sesame oil
- ½ cup watercress
- 3 tbsp chopped parsley
- Salt and freshly ground black pepper to taste
- Lemon wedges to garnish

Directions:

1. Pour cauliflower into a large safe-microwave bowl, sprinkle with some water, and steam in microwave for 1 to 2 minutes or until softened.

2. In a large salad bowl, combine cauliflower, tomatoes, olives, lemon zest and juice, green onions, almonds, goji berries, sesame oil, watercress, and parsley. Season

with salt and black pepper, and mix well.

3. Serve with lemon wedges.

Nutrition:

Calories 203, Total Fat 15.28g, Total Carbs 9.64g, Fiber 3.2g, Net Carbs 6.44g, Protein 6.67g, Protein 2.54g

Tofu-Dulse-Walnut Salad

Preparation Time: 10 minutes

Cooking Time: 15 minutes

Serving Size: 4

Ingredients:

- 1 (7 ozblock extra firm tofu
- 2 tbsp olive oil
- 2 tbsp butter
- 1 cup asparagus, trimmed and halved
- 1 cup green beans, trimmed
- 2 tbsp chopped dulse
- Salt and freshly ground black pepper to taste
- ½ lemon, juiced
- 4 tbsp chopped walnuts

Directions:

1. Place tofu in between two paper towels and allow soaking for 5 minutes. After, remove towels and chop into small cubes.
2. Heat olive oil in a skillet and fry tofu until golden, 10 minutes. Remove onto a paper towel-lined plate and set aside.
3. Melt butter in skillet and sauté asparagus and green beans until softened, 5 minutes. Add dulse, season with salt and black pepper, and Cooking Time: until softened. Mix in tofu and stir-fry for 5 minutes.

4. Plate, drizzle with lemon juice, and scatter walnuts on top.
5. Serve warm.

Nutrition:

Calories 237, Total Fat 19.57g, Total Carbs 5.9g, Fiber 2.1g, Net Carbs 3.89, Protein 12.75g

Warm Mushroom And Orange Pepper Salad

Preparation Time: 10 minutes

Cooking Time: 8 minutes

Serving Size: 4

Ingredients:

- 2 tbsp avocado oil
- 1 cup mixed mushrooms, chopped
- 2 orange bell peppers, deseeded and finely sliced
- 1 garlic clove, minced
- 2 tbsp tamarind sauce
- 1 tsp maple (sugar-freesyrup
- ½ tsp hot sauce
- ½ tsp fresh ginger paste
- Sesame seeds to garnish

Directions:

1. Over medium fire, heat half of avocado oil in a large skillet, sauté mushroom and bell peppers until slightly softened, 5 minutes.
2. In a small bowl, whisk garlic, tamarind sauce, maple syrup, hot sauce, and ginger paste. Add mixture to vegetables and stir-fry for 2 to 3 minutes.
3. Turn heat off and dish salad. Drizzle with remaining avocado oil and garnish with sesame seeds.
4. Serve with grilled tofu.

Nutrition:

Calories 289, Total Fat 26.71g, Total Carbs 9g, Fiber 3.8g, Net Carbs 5.2g, Protein 4.23g

SOUPS AND STEWS

Shiitake Mushroom Split Pea Soup

Preparation time: 10 minutes

Cooking time: 6 hours

Total time: 6 hours 10 minutes

Servings: 12

Ingredients:

- 1 cup dried, green split peas
- 2 cups celery, chopped
- 2 cups sliced carrots
- 1½ cups cauliflower, chopped
- 2 ounces dried shiitake mushrooms, chopped
- 9 ounces frozen artichoke hearts
- 11 cups water
- 1 teaspoon garlic powder
- 1½ teaspoon onion powder
- ½ teaspoon black pepper
- 1 tablespoon parsley
- ½ teaspoon ginger
- ½ teaspoon ground mustard seed
- ½ tablespoon brown rice vinegar

How to Prepare:

1. Add all the ingredients to a slow cooker.

2. Put on the slow cooker's lid and Cooking Time: for 6 hours on low heat.

3. Once done, garnish as desired.

4. Serve warm.

Nutritional Values:

Calories 361

Total Fat 16.3 g

Saturated Fat 4.9 g

Cholesterol 114 mg

Sodium 515 mg

Total Carbs 29.3 g

Fiber 0.1 g

Sugar 18.2 g

Protein 3.3 g

Spinach Soup With Basil

Preparation time: 10 minutes

Cooking time: 5hrs. 5 minutes

Total time: 5 hrs. 15 minutes

Servings: 06

Ingredients:

- 8 ounces potatoes, diced
- 1 medium onion, chopped
- 1 large clove of garlic, chopped
- 1 teaspoon powdered mustard
- 3 cups water
- ¼ teaspoon salt
- Ground cayenne pepper
- ½ cup packed fresh dill
- 10 ounces frozen spinach

How to Prepare:

1. In a low cooker, add olive oil and onion.
2. Sauté for 5 minutes then toss in rest of the soup ingredients.
3. Put on the slow cooker's lid and Cooking Time: for 5 hours on low heat.

4. Once done, puree the soup with a hand blender.

5. Serve warm.

Nutritional Values:

Calories 162

Total Fat 4 g

Saturated Fat 1.9 g

Cholesterol 25 mg

Sodium 101 mg

Total Carbs 17.8 g

Sugar 2.1 g

Fiber 6 g

Protein 4 g

Black-Eyed Pea Soup With Olive Pesto

Preparation time: 10 minutes

Cooking time: 3 hrs. 5 minutes

Total time: 3 hrs. 15 minutes

Servings: 04

Ingredients:

Soup:

- 1 leek, trimmed
- 1 tablespoon olive oil
- 1 clove garlic, chopped
- 1 small carrot, chopped
- 1 stem fresh thyme, chopped
- 1 (15 ouncecan black-eyed peas, drained and rinsed
- 2½ cups vegetable broth
- ½ teaspoon salt
- ¼ teaspoon black pepper

Pesto:

- 1¼ cups pitted green olives
- ¼ cup parsley leaves
- 1 clove garlic
- 1 teaspoon capers, drained
- 1 tablespoon olive oil

How to Prepare:

1. In a slow cooker, add olive oil, carrot, leek, and garlic.
2. Sauté for 5 minutes then toss in the rest of the soup ingredients.
3. Put on the slow cooker's lid and Cooking Time: for 3 hours on low heat.
4. Meanwhile, blend the pesto ingredients in a blender until smooth.
5. Blend the soup in the slow cooker with a hand mixer.
6. Top with prepared pesto.
7. Serve warm.

Nutritional Values:

Calories 72

Total Fat 15.4 g

Saturated Fat 4.2 g

Cholesterol 168 mg

Sodium 203 mg

Total Carbs 28.5 g

Sugar 1.1 g

Fiber 4 g

Protein 7.9 g

Beanless Garden Soup

Preparation time: 10 minutes

Cooking time: 4 hrs. 5 minutes

Total time: 4 hrs. 15 minutes

Servings: 04

Ingredients:

- 1 medium onion, diced
- 2 cloves garlic, minced
- 1 green bell pepper, diced
- 1 red bell pepper, diced
- 2 carrots, peeled and diced
- 1 medium zucchini, diced
- 1 small eggplant, diced
- 1 hot banana pepper, seeded and minced
- 1 jalapeño pepper, seeded and minced
- 1 can (28 ouncediced tomatoes
- 3 cups vegetable broth
- 1½ tablespoon chili powder
- 2 teaspoons smoked paprika
- 1 tablespoon cumin
- 2 tablespoons fresh oregano, chopped
- 2 tablespoons fresh cilantro, chopped
- Salt and black pepper to taste
- A few dashes of liquid smoke

How to Prepare:

1. In a slow cooker, add olive oil and onion.
2. Sauté for 5 minutes then toss in the rest of the ingredients.
3. Put on the slow cooker's lid and Cooking Time: for 4 hours on low heat.
4. Once done mix well.
5. Serve warm.

Nutritional Values:

Calories 305

Total Fat 11.8 g

Saturated Fat 2.2 g

Cholesterol 56 mg

Sodium 321 mg

Total Carbs 34.6 g

Fibers 0.4 g

Sugar 2 g

Protein 7 g

Caldo Verde A La Mushrooms

Preparation time: 10 minutes

Cooking time: 5 hrs. 5 minutes

Total time: 5 hrs. 15 minutes

Servings: 08

Ingredients:

- ¼ cup olive oil
- 10 ounces button mushrooms, cleaned, and sliced
- 1½ teaspoons smoked paprika
- 1 pinch ground cayenne pepper
- 1 teaspoon salt
- 1 large onion, diced
- 2 cloves garlic, minced
- 2 pounds russet potatoes, peeled and diced
- 7 cups vegetable broth
- 8 ounces kale, sliced
- ½ teaspoon black pepper

How to Prepare:

1. In a pan, heat cooking oil and sauté mushrooms for 12 minutes.
2. Season the mushrooms with salt, cayenne pepper, and paprika.
3. Add olive oil and onion to a slow cooker.
4. Sauté for 5 minutes then toss in rest of the soup

ingredients.

5. Put on the slow cooker's lid and Cooking Time: for 5 hours on low heat.

6. Once done, puree the soup with a hand blender.

7. Stir in sautéed mushrooms.

8. Serve.

Nutritional Values:

Calories 231

Total Fat 20.1 g

Saturated Fat 2.4 g

Cholesterol 110 mg

Sodium 941 mg

Total Carbs 20.1 g

Fiber 0.9 g

Sugar 1.4 g

Protein 4.6 g

Black-Eyed Pea Soup With Greens

Preparation time: 10 minutes

Cooking time: 5 hrs.

Total time: 5 hrs. 10 minutes

Servings: 04

Ingredients:

- ½ cup black eyed peas
- ½ cup brown lentils
- 1 teaspoon oil
- ½ teaspoon cumin seeds
- ½ cup onions, chopped
- 5 cloves garlic, chopped
- 1-inch piece of ginger chopped
- 1 teaspoon ground coriander
- ½ teaspoon ground cumin
- ½ teaspoon turmeric
- ¼ teaspoon black pepper
- ½ teaspoon cayenne powder
- 2 tomatoes, chopped
- ½ teaspoon lemon juice
- 1 teaspoon salt
- 2 ½ cups water
- ½ cup chopped spinach
- ½ cup small chopped green beans

How to Prepare:

1. Add olive oil and cumin seeds to a slow cooker.
2. Sauté for 1 minute then toss in the rest of the ingredients.
3. Put on the slow cooker's lid and Cooking Time: for 5 hours on low heat.
4. Once done, garnish as desired
5. Serve warm.

Nutritional Values:

Calories 197

Total Fat 4 g

Saturated Fat 0.5 g

Cholesterol 135 mg

Sodium 790 mg

Total Carbs 31 g

Fiber 12.2 g

Sugar 2.5 g

Protein 11 g

Sweet Potato And Peanut Soup

Preparation time: 10 minutes

Cooking time: 4 hrs. 5 minutes

Total time: 4 hrs. 15 minutes

Servings: 06

Ingredients:

- 1 tablespoon water
- 6 cups sweet potatoes, peeled and chopped
- 2 cups onions, chopped
- 1 cup celery, chopped
- 4 large cloves garlic, chopped
- 1 teaspoon salt
- 2 teaspoons cumin seeds
- 3½ teaspoons ground coriander
- 1 teaspoon paprika
- ½ teaspoon crushed red pepper flakes
- 2 cups vegetable stock
- 3 cups water
- 4 tablespoons fresh ginger, grated
- 2 tablespoons natural peanut butter
- 2 cups cooked chickpeas
- 4 tablespoons lime juice
- Fresh cilantro, chopped
- Chopped peanuts, to garnish

How to Prepare:

1. In a slow cooker, add olive oil and onion.

2. Sauté for 5 minutes then toss in the rest of the soup ingredients except chickpeas.

3. Put on the slow cooker's lid and Cooking Time: for 4 hours on low heat.

4. Once done, blend the soup with a hand blender.

5. Stir in chickpeas and garnish with cilantro and peanuts.

6. Serve warm.

Nutritional Values:

Calories 201

Total Fat 8.9 g

Saturated Fat 4.5 g

Cholesterol 57 mg

Sodium 340 mg

Total Carbs 24.7 g

Fiber 1.2 g

Sugar 1.3 g

Protein 15.3 g

Red Lentil Salsa Soup

Preparation time: 10 minutes

Cooking time: 17 minutes

Total time: 27 minutes

Servings: 06

Ingredients:

- 1¼ cups red lentils, rinsed
- 4 cups of water
- ½ cup diced red bell pepper
- 1¼ cups red salsa
- 1 tablespoon chili powder
- 1 tablespoon dried oregano
- 1 teaspoon smoked paprika
- ¼ teaspoon black pepper
- ¾ cup frozen sweet corn
- Salt to taste
- 2 tablespoons lime juice

How to Prepare:

1. In a saucepan, add all the ingredients except the corn.
2. Put on saucepan's lid and Cooking Time: for 15 minutes at a simmer.
3. Stir in corn and Cooking Time: for another 2 minutes.
4. Serve.

Nutritional Values:

Calories 119

Total Fat 14 g

Saturated Fat 2 g

Cholesterol 65 mg

Sodium 269 mg

Total Carbs 19 g

Fiber 4 g

Sugar 6 g

Protein 5g

Velvety Vegetable Soup

Preparation time: 10 minutes

Cooking time: 2hrs 2 minutes

Total time: 2 hrs. 12 minutes

Servings: 4

Ingredients:

- ½ sweet onion, chopped
- 4 garlic cloves, chopped
- 1 small head broccoli, chopped
- 2 stalks celery, chopped
- 1 cup green peas
- 3 green onions, chopped
- 2¾ cups vegetable broth
- 4 cups leafy greens
- 1 (15 ouncecan of cannellini beans
- Juice from 1 lemon
- 2 tablespoons fresh dill, chopped
- 5 fresh mint leaves
- 1 teaspoon salt
- ½ cup coconut milk
- Fresh herbs and peas, to garnish

How to Prepare:

1. In a slow cooker, add olive oil and onion.
2. Sauté for 2 minutes then toss in the rest of the soup

ingredients.

3. Put on the slow cooker's lid and Cooking Time: for 2 hours on low heat.

4. Once done, blend the soup with a hand blender.

5. Garnish with fresh herbs and peas.

6. Serve warm.

Nutritional Values:

Calories 205

Total Fat 22.7 g

Saturated Fat 6.1 g

Cholesterol 4 mg

Sodium 227 mg

Total Carbs 26.1 g

Fiber 1.4 g

Sugar 0.9 g

Protein 5.2 g

Ingredient Lentil Soup

Preparation Time: 50 minutes

Servings: 2

Ingredients

- Brown lentils: 1 ¼ cups
- Fresh rosemary leaves: 2 ½ tbsp minced
- Onion: 1 large chopped
- Sea salt: as per your taste
- Black pepper: ¼ tsp
- Water: 6 cups

Directions:

1. Take a large saucepan and add 1/3 cup of water and bring to boil
2. Add the chopped onions and lower the heat to medium
3. Stir with intervals for 10 minutes till onion changes color
4. Add salt, pepper, and rosemary and continue to stir for a minutes
5. Add lentils and remaining water to the pan and cover and Cooking Time: for 20 minutes
6. Lower the heat and continue simmering for 15 more minutes
7. Stir and break some lentils in the final minutes
8. Blend the soup if you like a creamy texture
9. Add more salt and pepper if needed and serve

Nutrition:

Carbs: 20 g

Protein: 8.5 g

Fats: 0.4 g

Calories: 150 Kcal

Ingredient Carrot And Red Lentil Soup

Preparation Time: 40 minutes

Servings: 3

Ingredients

- Split red lentils: 1 cup
- Carrots: 1 cup grated
- Water: 6 cups
- Onion: 1 large coarsely chopped
- Fine sea salt: as per your taste

Directions:

1. Take a large saucepan and add water and bring to boil
2. Add the chopped onions, carrots, lentils and salt and bring to boil
3. Lower the heat to medium and Cooking Time: for 20 minutes with partial cover
4. Add the mixture to the high-speed blender to make a puree
5. Whisk in water if desired
6. Add again to the pan and slowly heat on a low flame for 10-15 minutes
7. Add herbs or spices in between to augment the taste

Nutrition:

Carbs: 15.3 g

Protein: 6.2 g

Fats: 0.3 g

Calories: 90 Kcal

Ingredient Enchilada Soup

Preparation Time: 25 minutes

Servings: 3

Ingredients

- Tomatoes: 1 cup crushed
- Vegan red enchilada sauce: 1.5 cups
- Black beans: 2 cups can rinsed and drained

Directions:

1. Take a medium-sized saucepan and add crushed tomatoes and enchilada sauce
2. Heat on a medium flame to thicken it for 6-8 minutes
3. Add beans to the pan and lower the heat to a minimum
4. Cooking Time: for 8-10 minutes
5. Serve with any toppings if you like

Nutrition:

Carbs: 27.4 g

Protein: 11g

Fats: 1 g

Calories: 166.4 Kcal

SAUCES, AND CONDIMENTS

Potato Carrot Gravy

Preparation Time: 20 Minutes

Servings: 2 cups of gravy

Ingredients:

- 1 potato, peeled and chopped
- ½ lb (about 4carrots, chopped
- 2 cups water
- 1 tsp garlic powder
- 1 tsp onion powder
- 1 tsp salt
- 1/2 tsp turmeric
- 2 tbsp nutritional yeast
- 2 tsp soy sauce

Directions:

1. Add potato and carrot to Instant Pot along with water.
2. Cover the pot with lid. Set steam release handle to 'sealing' and switch on manual button for 7 minutes over high-pressure.
3. When the timer beeps, allow it to naturally release steam for 5 minutes and then change stem handle to 'venting' to release any remaining steam.
4. Add in rest of the ingredients to Instant Pot® and using

an immersion blender, make gravy directly in Instant Pot.

5. To make the gravy thinner just add a bit more water.

Barbecue Sauce

Preparation time: 5 minutes

Cooking time: 0 minute

Servings: 16

Ingredients:

- 8 ounces tomato sauce
- 1 teaspoon garlic powder
- ¼ teaspoon ground black pepper
- 1/2 teaspoon. sea salt
- 2 Tablespoons Dijon mustard
- 3 packets stevia
- 1 teaspoon molasses
- 1 Tablespoon apple cider vinegar
- 2 Tablespoons tamari
- 1 teaspoon liquid aminos

Directions:

1. Take a medium bowl, place all the ingredients in it, and stir until combined.
2. Serve straight away

Nutrition Value:

Calories: 29 Cal

Fat: 0.1 g

Carbs: 7 g

Protein: 0.1 g

Fiber: 0.1 g

Garden Pesto

Preparation time: 5 minutes

Cooking time: 0 minute

Servings: 10

Ingredients:

- 1/4 cup pistachios, shelled
- 3/4 cup parsley leaves
- 1 cup cilantro leaves
- ½ teaspoon minced garlic
- 1/4 cup mint leaves
- 1 cup basil leaves
- ¼ teaspoon ground black pepper
- 1/3 teaspoon salt
- 1/2 cup olive oil
- 1 1/2 teaspoons miso
- 2 teaspoons lemon juice

Directions:

1. Place all the ingredients in the order in a food processor or blender and then pulse for 3 to 5 minutes at high speed until smooth.
2. Tip the pesto in a bowl and then serve.

Nutrition Value:

Calories: 111.5 Cal

Fat: 11.5 g

Carbs: 2.8 g

Protein: 1.2 g

Fiber: 1.4 g

Alfredo Sauce

Preparation time: 5 minutes

Cooking time: 0 minute

Servings: 4

Ingredients:

- 1 cup cashews, unsalted, soaked in warm water for 15 minutes
- 1 teaspoon minced garlic
- 1/4 teaspoon ground black pepper
- 1/3 teaspoon salt
- 1/4 cup nutritional yeast
- 2 tablespoons tamari
- 2 tablespoons olive oil
- 4 tablespoons water

Directions:

1. Drain the cashews, transfer them into a food processor, add remaining ingredients in it, and pulse for 3 minutes until thick sauce comes together.
2. Serve straight away.

Nutrition Value:

Calories: 105.7 Cal

Fat: 5.3 g

Carbs: 11 g

Protein: 4.7 g

Fiber: 2 g

Creamy Cheesy Sauce

Preparation Time: 6 Minutes

Servings: 2 cups

Ingredients:

- 1cup cashews, soaked
- ½teaspoon vegetable broth powder
- 1teaspoon Dijon mustard
- ½teaspoon paprika
- ½teaspoon garlic powder
- 2tablespoons fresh lemon juice
- ½teaspoon salt
- ½cup nutritional yeast
- 1cup almond milk
- ½teaspoon onion powder

Directions:

1. Add the cashews in a blender.
2. Add the mustard, lemon juice, yeast, onion, salt, garlic, paprika, broth powder and blend into a smooth paste.
3. Serve with curry.

Bolognese Sauce

Preparation time: 10 minutes

Cooking time: 45 minutes

Servings: 8

Ingredients:

- ½ of small green bell pepper, chopped
- 1 stalk of celery, chopped
- 1 small carrot, chopped
- 1 medium white onion, peeled, chopped
- 2 teaspoons minced garlic
- 1/2 teaspoon crushed red pepper flakes
- 3 tablespoons olive oil
- 8-ounce tempeh, crumbled
- 8 ounces white mushrooms, chopped
- 1/2 cup dried red lentils
- 28-ounce crushed tomatoes
- 28-ounce whole tomatoes, chopped
- 1 teaspoon dried oregano
- 1/2 teaspoon fennel seed
- 1/2 teaspoon ground black pepper
- 1/2 teaspoon salt
- 1 teaspoon dried basil
- 1/4 cup chopped parsley
- 1 bay leaf

- 6-ounce tomato paste
- 1 cup dry red wine

Directions:

1. Take a Dutch oven, place it over medium heat, add oil, and when hot, add the first six ingredients, stir and Cooking Time: for 5 minutes until sauté.

2. Then switch heat to medium-high level, add two ingredients after olive oil, stir and Cooking Time: for 3 minutes.

3. Switch heat to medium-low level, stir in tomato paste, and continue cooking for 2 minutes.

4. Add remaining ingredients except for lentils, stir and bring the mixture to boil.

5. Switch heat to the low level, simmer sauce for 10 minutes, covering the pan partially, then add lentils and continue cooking for 20 minutes until tender.

6. Serve sauce with cooked pasta.

Nutrition Value:

Calories: 208.8 Cal

Fat: 12 g

Carbs: 17.8 g

Protein: 10.6 g

Fiber: 3.8 g

Cilantro And Parsley Hot Sauce

Preparation time: 5 minutes

Cooking time: 0 minute

Servings: 4

Ingredients:

- 2 cups of parsley and cilantro leaves with stems
- 4 Thai bird chilies, destemmed, deseeded, torn
- 2 teaspoons minced garlic
- 1 teaspoon salt
- 1/4 teaspoon coriander seed, ground
- 1/4 teaspoon ground black pepper
- 1/2 teaspoon cumin seeds, ground
- 3 green cardamom pods, toasted, ground
- 1/2 cup olive oil

Directions:

1. Take a spice blender or a food processor, place all the ingredients in it, and process for 5 minutes until the smooth paste comes together.
2. Serve straight away.

Nutrition Value:

Calories: 130 Cal

Fat: 14 g

Carbs: 2 g

Protein: 1 g

Fiber: 1 g

Mushroom Gravy

Preparation Time: 20 Minutes

Servings: 10

Ingredients:

- 2 cups sliced fresh mushrooms
- 1½ cups plus 2 tablespoons vegetable or mushroom broth
- 2 tablespoons dry red or white wine
- ¼ cup minced yellow onion
- ½ teaspoon ground dried thyme
- ¼ teaspoon ground sage
- Salt and freshly ground black pepper
- ½ to 1 teaspoon vegan gravy browner

Directions:

1. Combine the onion and 2 tablespoons of broth in the open instant pot on low and simmer until the onion softens.
2. Add the mushrooms and soften more before adding the sage, thyme, and wine.
3. Add half the broth and boil.
4. Reduce the heat and simmer 5 minutes.
5. Add the remaining broth, then put into a blender and make smooth.
6. Put back into the instant pot, salt and pepper, then seal and Cooking Time: on Stew for 10 minutes.

7. Depressurize naturally and serve hot.

Healthy One-Pot Hummus

Preparation Time: 1 HR 15 Minutes

Servings: 2

Ingredients:

- 1 cup dry garbanzo beans
- 2 cups water
- ½ tsp salt
- 1 tsp cumin
- 2 garlic cloves
- Juice of ½ lemon

Directions:

1. Rinse and drain garbanzo beans. Add beans and water to Instant Pot and Cooking Time: for 1 hour over manual setting, high pressure. Set steam release handle to 'sealing'.
2. When the timer beeps, using quick release Directions, release the steam immediately.
3. Place garbanzo beans along with remaining ingredients in a blender. Use the reserved water after cooking beans.
4. Blend the mixture over high until creamy smooth and serve.

Instant Pot Sriracha Sauce

Preparation Time: 30 Minutes

Servings: 2 cups of Sriracha

Ingredients:

- 1 lb red chili peppers (jalapeno, Fresno, etc.
- 6 garlic cloves, peeled
- ½ cup distilled vinegar
- 3 tbsp brown sugar
- 1/3 cup water
- 1 tbsp salt

Directions:

1. Chop chili peppers and put them into a blender.
2. Add remaining ingredients into the blender and blend over high until smooth.
3. Pour this mixture into Instant Pot. Switch on sautée button. Then set 'Adjust' button two times to change heat setting to 'Less'.
4. Let the mixture sauté for about 15 minutes stirring occasionally. After 15 minutes, allow the sauce to cool for about 15 minutes.
5. Store the sriracha in glass containers and keep it in the fridge for 2 weeks.

SNACKS

Tomato And Pesto Toast

Preparation Time: 5 minutes

Cooking Time: 0 minute

Servings: 4

Ingredients:

- 1 small tomato, sliced
- ¼ teaspoon ground black pepper
- 1 tablespoon vegan pesto
- 2 tablespoons hummus
- 1 slice of whole-grain bread, toasted
- Hemp seeds as needed for garnishing

Directions:

1. Spread hummus on one side of the toast, top with tomato slices and then drizzle with pesto.
2. Sprinkle black pepper on the toast along with hemp seeds and then serve straight away.

Nutrition:

Calories: 214 Cal

Fat: 7.2 g

Carbs: 32 g

Protein: 6.5 g

Fiber: 3 g

Carrot And Sweet Potato Fritters

Preparation Time: 10 minutes

Cooking Time: 8 minutes

Servings: 10

Ingredients:

- 1/3 cup quinoa flour
- 1½ cups shredded sweet potato
- 1 cup grated carrot
- 1/3 teaspoon ground black pepper
- 2/3 teaspoon salt
- 2 teaspoons curry powder
- 2 flax eggs
- 2 tablespoons coconut oil

Directions:

1. Place all the ingredients in a bowl, except for oil, stir well until combined and then shape the mixture into ten small patties
2. Take a large pan, place it over medium-high heat, add oil and when it melts, add patties in it and Cooking Time: for 3 minutes per side until browned.
3. Serve straight away

Nutrition:

Calories: 70 Cal

Fat: 3 g

Carbs: 8 g

Protein: 1 g

Fiber: 1 g

Chipotle And Lime Tortilla Chips

Preparation Time: 10 minutes

Cooking Time: 15 minutes

Servings: 4

Ingredients:

- 12 ounces whole-wheat tortillas
- 4 tablespoons chipotle seasoning
- 1 tablespoon olive oil
- 4 limes, juiced

Directions:

1. Whisk together oil and lime juice, brush it well on tortillas, then sprinkle with chipotle seasoning and bake for 15 minutes at 350 degrees F until crispy, turning halfway.

2. When done, let the tortilla cool for 10 minutes, then break it into chips and serve.

Nutrition:

Calories: 150 Cal

Fat: 7 g

Carbs: 18 g

Protein: 2 g

Fiber: 2 g

Zucchini Hummus

Preparation Time: 5 minutes

Cooking Time: 0 minute

Servings: 8

Ingredients:

- 1 cup diced zucchini
- 1/2 teaspoon sea salt
- 1 teaspoon minced garlic
- 2 teaspoons ground cumin
- 3 tablespoons lemon juice
- 1/3 cup tahini

Directions:

1. Place all the ingredients in a food processor and pulse for 2 minutes until smooth.
2. Tip the hummus in a bowl, drizzle with oil and serve.

Nutrition:

Calories: 65 Cal

Fat: 5 g

Carbs: 3 g

Protein: 2 g

Fiber: 1 g

Avocado And Sprout Toast

Preparation Time: 5 minutes

Cooking Time: 0 minute

Servings: 4

Ingredients:

- 1/2 of a medium avocado, sliced
- 1 slice of whole-grain bread, toasted
- 2 tablespoons sprouts
- 2 tablespoons hummus
- ¼ teaspoon lemon zest
- ½ teaspoon hemp seeds
- ¼ teaspoon red pepper flakes

Directions:

1. Spread hummus on one side of the toast and then top with avocado slices and sprouts.
2. Sprinkle with lemon zest, hemp seeds, and red pepper flakes and then serve straight away.

Nutrition:

Calories: 200 Cal

Fat: 10.5 g

Carbs: 22 g

Protein: 7 g

Fiber: 7 g

DESSERT AND DRINKS

Chocolate Cookies

Preparation time: 10 minutes

Cooking time: 25 minutes

Servings: 12

Ingredients:

- 1 teaspoon vanilla extract
- ½ cup coconut butter, melted
- 1 tablespoon flax meal combined with 2 tablespoons water
- 4 tablespoons coconut sugar
- 2 cups flour
- ½ cup unsweetened vegan chocolate chips

Directions:

1. In a bowl, mix flax meal with vanilla extract and sugar and stir well.
2. Add melted butter, flour and half of the chocolate chips and stir everything.
3. Transfer this to a pan that fits your air fryer, spread the rest of the chocolate chips on top, introduce in the fryer at 330 degrees F and bake for 25 minutes.
4. Slice when it's cold and serve.
5. Enjoy!

Nutrition: calories 230, fat 12, fiber 2, carbs 13, protein 5

Coconut And Seeds Bars

Preparation time: 10 minutes

Cooking time: 35 minutes

Servings: 4

Ingredients:

- 1 cup coconut, shredded
- ½ cup almonds
- ½ cup pecans, chopped
- 2 tablespoons coconut sugar
- ½ cup pumpkin seeds
- ½ cup sunflower seeds
- 2 tablespoons sunflower oil
- 1 teaspoon nutmeg, ground
- 1 teaspoon pumpkin pie spice

Directions:

1. In a bowl, mix almonds and pecans with pumpkin seeds, sunflower seeds, coconut, nutmeg and pie spice and stir well.
2. Heat up a pan with the oil over medium heat, add sugar, stir well, pour this over nuts and coconut mix and stir well.
3. Spread this on a lined baking sheet that fits your air fryer, introduce in your air fryer and Cooking Time: at 300 degrees F and bake for 25 minutes.
4. Leave the mix aside to cool down, cut and serve.

5. Enjoy!

Nutrition: calories 252, fat 7, fiber 8, carbs 12, protein 7

Blueberry Cake

Preparation time: 10 minutes

Cooking time: 30 minutes

Servings: 6

Ingredients:

- ½ cup whole wheat flour
- ¼ teaspoon baking powder
- ¼ teaspoon stevia
- ¼ cup blueberries
- 1/3 cup almond milk
- 1 teaspoon olive oil
- 1 teaspoon flaxseed, ground
- ½ teaspoon lemon zest, grated
- ¼ teaspoon vanilla extract
- ¼ teaspoon lemon extract
- Cooking spray

Directions:

1. In a bowl, mix flour with baking powder, stevia, blueberries, milk, oil, flaxseeds, lemon zest, vanilla extract and lemon extract and whisk well.
2. Spray a cake pan with cooking spray, line it with parchment paper, pour cake batter, introduce in the

fryer and Cooking Time: at 350 degrees F for 30 minutes.

3. Leave the cake to cool down, slice and serve.

4. Enjoy!

Nutrition: calories 210, fat 4, fiber 4, carbs 10, protein 4

Simple And Sweet Bananas

Preparation time: 10 minutes

Cooking time: 15 minutes

Servings: 4

Ingredients:

- 3 tablespoons coconut butter
- 2 tablespoons flax meal combined with 2 tablespoons water
- 8 bananas, peeled and halved
- ½ cup corn flour
- 3 tablespoons cinnamon powder
- 1 cup vegan breadcrumbs

Directions:

1. Heat up a pan with the butter over medium-high heat, add breadcrumbs, stir and Cooking Time: for 4 minutes and then transfer to a bowl.
2. Roll each banana in flour, flax meal and breadcrumbs mix.
3. Arrange bananas in your air fryer's basket, dust with cinnamon sugar and Cooking Time: at 280 degrees F for 10 minutes.
4. Transfer to plates and serve.
5. Enjoy!

Nutrition: calories 214, fat 1, fiber 4, carbs 12, protein 4

Almond And Vanilla Cake

Preparation time: 10 minutes

Cooking time: 30 minutes

Servings: 8

Ingredients:

- 1 and ½ cup stevia
- 1 cup flour
- ¼ cup cocoa powder+ 2 tablespoons
- ½ cup chocolate almond milk
- 2 teaspoons baking powder
- 2 tablespoons canola oil
- 1 teaspoon vanilla extract
- 1 and ½ cups hot water
- Cooking spray

Directions:

1. In a bowl, mix flour with 2 tablespoons cocoa, baking powder, almond milk, oil and vanilla extract, whisk well and spread on the bottom of a cake pan greased with cooking spray.
2. In a separate bowl, mix stevia with the rest of the cocoa and the water, whisk well and spread over the batter in the pan.
3. Introduce in the fryer and Cooking Time: at 350 degrees F for 30 minutes.
4. Leave the cake to cool down, slice and serve.

5. Enjoy!

Nutrition: calories 250, fat 4, fiber 3, carbs 10, protein 2

Coffee Pudding

Preparation time: 10 minutes

Cooking time: 10 minutes

Servings: 4

Ingredients:

- 4 ounces coconut butter
- 4 ounces dark vegan chocolate, chopped
- Juice of ½ orange
- 1 teaspoon baking powder
- 2 ounces whole wheat flour
- ½ teaspoon instant coffee
- 2 tablespoons flax meal combined with 2 tablespoons water
- 2 ounces coconut sugar

Directions:

1. Heat up a pan with the coconut butter over medium heat, add chocolate and orange juice, stir well and take off heat.
2. In a bowl, mix sugar with instant coffee and flax meal, beat using your mixer, add chocolate mix, flour, salt and baking powder and stir well.
3. Pour this into a greased pan, introduce in your air fryer, Cooking Time: at 360 degrees F for 10 minutes, divide between plates and serve.
4. Enjoy!

Nutrition: calories 189, fat 6, fiber 4, carbs 14, protein 3

Apple And Honey Toast

Preparation Time: 5 minutes

Cooking Time: 0 minute

Servings: 4

Ingredients:

- ½ of a small apple, cored, sliced
- 1 slice of whole-grain bread, toasted
- 1 tablespoon honey
- 2 tablespoons hummus
- 1/8 teaspoon cinnamon

Directions:

1. Spread hummus on one side of the toast, top with apple slices and then drizzle with honey.
2. Sprinkle cinnamon on it and then serve straight away.

Nutrition:

Calories: 212 Cal

Fat: 7 g

Carbs: 35 g

Protein: 4 g

Fiber: 5.5 g

CPSIA information can be obtained
at www.ICGtesting.com
Printed in the USA
LVHW021735250421
685459LV00001B/288